PARADISE LOST; ENGLISH GAINED PART - II

A COLLECTION OF MILTONIC EXPRESSIONS

M.A. MOHAMED SAHUL HAMEED

Made with ♥ on the Notion Press Platform
www.notionpress.com

Contents

About The Authors

Dr. M.A. Mohamed Sahul Hameed, Dr. R. Srinivasan and Dr. G. Christopher are currently serving as members of faculty in the Department of English, Vellore Institute of Technology, Vellore. They have more than two and a half decades of teaching experience. This book is the outcome of their quest for language and literature. They have published many research articles both in language and literature in international journals of repute, and they have produced many PhD scholars in English. They are of the belief that literature will ever remain as a unique tool for developing language abilities.

Acknowledgements

Being a believer myself, I offer my sincere prayers to God for His greatest blessings upon me!

At the outset, I wish to express my heartfelt thanks to my beloved parents Janab Abdur Rahman and Janaba Hajaral Beevi, who, I do feel, are with me for ever, praying for me even after their leaving this earth. My dedicating this book to my beloved parents is nothing before their care and concern that they were bestowing upon me till the end of their life.

I place on record my heartfelt thanks to our Hon'ble Chancellor Dr G.Viswanathan, our respected Vice-Presidents Mr Sankar Viswanathan, Dr Sekar Viswanathan and Mr G.V.Selvam for their constant support and encouragement in bringing this book to light.

I am greatly indebted to my belov'd colleagues Dr R.Srinivasan and Dr G. Christopher, Dept of English for their kind consent to be the co-authors of this book and for their commendable contributions to this book.

I express a great deal of gratitude to my wife Yasmin and my belov'd daughter Sajitha Hajr for sparing their time with me, motivating me to bring this book to light.

My heartfelt thanks are due to my belov'd son M.S. Abdur Rahman for designing the cover page of the book, making all page alignments and helping me in bringing this book expeditiously to light.

I thank all my friends, well-wishers, relatives and students for encouraging me a lot to bring this book out.

CHAPTER ONE

INTRODUCTION

Heard melodies are sweet, but those unheard are sweeter. The treasures of Literature-read are great and those unread, unfound, and uninterrupted might be greater. The world might not have been visible to John Milton, but John Milton has always been visible to the world. Paradise might have been lost, but English was gained. Satan might have fallen from God's grace, but English did not fall from Milton's grace.

'Paradise Lost' is an epic poem in blank verse written by John Milton, a great English poet of the 17th century but a standing poet of every century. John Milton with his poetic eyes had a clear vision and penned the image of Paradise in his won ways and presented to the world in beautiful English. Paradise might have been lost or regained, but the World of Literature gained a lot.

The hungry edge of appetite cannot be cloyed by bare imagination of a royal feast, and the quest for the English language cannot be quenched without the treasures of literature. No language can be thought of in its full and unique, innovative, impressive, productive, constructive forms without literature. The taste of language can be enjoyed and experienced through literature.

John Milton said, "I wish to leave something which the posterity will not willingly let die." Great writers live through their works for ever even after death.

The purpose of the authors having written this book is neither to discover any new paradise nor to regain the paradise lost, but to make visible some of the great expressions in English written by a great poet, to whom nothing was visible, to the slow learners of English and to enable them to use Miltonic expressions in their day-to-day conversation and communication. The expressions have been taken from Milton's Paradise Lost-Book III& IV. Each expression is followed by a few sample sentences. Whether there are minds to be changed by place or time, there could hopefully be at least a few minds to be impressed and illuminated with Miltonic expressions. A very few have been placed before the young learners, and perhaps, they could explore more.

- Authors

CHAPTER TWO

EXPRESSIONS AND EXPLANATIONS OF BOOK III

- ....in unapproached light

(Is God unapproached? Or is God unapproachable? For the non-believers, there is no need for any answer. Such questions and any answer, to them, might seem to be illogical or ridiculous. But for those who strongly believe in God, God is approachable, but He is not approached with faith or He is approached only at the time of crisis. Is it the Light that removes darkness? Is it the Light that illuminates our life? Is it the Light that leads us towards light? Once a non-believer was asked by a theist what he would do if he were shown God, and the non-believer r
eplied that he would start believing in God.

If God were easily approachable, would Man keep God in high esteem? Does not familiarity breed contempt? It is also said that God responds quickly to the calls of those who do not believe in Him, but He delays His responses to the pious, for He tests their patience. It is believed that God helps the non-believers, but will forsake them, and that He might not help the believers, but will never forsake them. All these are beliefs, and no belief can be scientifically proved. Faith in God is beyond science and logic. Faith in God must be unshakable.

The people of a village were suffering a lot due to water scarcity, and there was no rain for years together. They decided to have a group prayer for rain. A date was fixed for the purpose, and on the date, all villagers gathered in the place for group prayer, but only one among a number of villagers had come there with an umbrella. That is Faith in God. So God is approachable, but unapproached.)

God is approachable, but unapproached.

The new professor appointed in our university is a highly informative book not read by many and a light unapproached.

The light, though unapproached, is shedding its light.

The world would not have seen the darkness, had the light remained unapproached.

The light is invisible as it is unapproached.

The hot summer makes us feel that the sunlight must remain unapproached.

- ....roll in vain

To find thy piercing ray, ...
(What is the use of rolling in vain without faith in God? God's piercing ray could be felt even in the dark but the perilous ray of Satan has its own ill-effects. The piercing rays in the eyes of young beautiful girls attract the eyes, minds and hearts of the teenagers. Many of us might have experienced the power of the piercing rays in the eyes of some of the Saints who are closer to God with their minds, hearts and souls. To avoid the piercing rays of the sun, many of us wear the sun glasses.

The poor are rolling in vain to find the piercing rays of the Creator in order to pray for some light in their lives.

With your piercing rays of your eyes, you try to find all your ways.

The Romeo of our street lost his eyes by continuously finding his Juliet's piercing rays of eyes.

With impure thoughts in mind and heart and with sinful acts aplenty, many of us are rolling in vain to enjoy the Heavenly piercing rays.

Unable to bear the piercing rays in her eyes, I keep my eyes always closed.

- ....equalled with me in fate,

(We find less number of people equalled in love, compassion and mercy, but we find a large number of people equalled in selfishness, arrogance and cruelty. Time makes such arrogant, selfish and cruel people equalled in fate. Is it one's fate that makes one suffer? Is it one's fate that makes one starve? But the word 'Fate' is being frequently used by many of us whenever we are plagued by misfortunes. Does 'Fate' play in one's life just because of one's sins in one's previous birth? If so, has it been proved by any even once? Or is it our failure to make plans in life? In what form does Fate appear in one's life? Why should Fate play with particular people's life, leaving all others happy? Adam was equalled with Eve in fate, for Fate played in Eve's life through Satan. Adam also fell a prey to fate. Adam and Eve were thrown out of the heavenly abode. Is it because of their disobedience? Or is it because of Fate? Did Fate advise Adam and Eve to disobey the command of God? Why did Fate not advise Satan not to disobey the command of God? Is is Satan's strength over Fate or is it Man's weakness over Fate? Whatever it is, Fate makes us look for reasons for blaming something or someone for all wrong deeds of ours.)

The second daughter-in-law is also equalled with the first daughter-in-law in fate.

There is no need for any angel to suffer equalled with any devil in fate.

The bond between the couple is so emotional and strong that they are found and they wish to be found equalled in fate and favour, fortune or misfortune, pleasure or pain, ups or downs.

When the new govt is formed, the corrupt officer will be equalled with the corrupt minister in fate.

He says that it is his fate that he is equalled with his rival in fate.

- **So were I equalled with them in renown.**

(Maria Salomea Sklodowska-Curie known simply as Marie Curie (1867-1934), a Polish and naturalist-French physicist and her husband Pierre Curie were equalled in renown. She won the Nobel Prize twice and her husband was the co-winner of her first Nobel Prize. She conducted pioneering research on radioactivity. On marriage occasions, people wish the couple in many ways, saying that they must live like Tom and his wife, Jack and his wife and Harry and his wife, but a couple must live like Marie Curie and Pierre Curie, for they were equalled not only in happiness, but also in renown.)

The child desires that she be equalled with every leader in renown.

Were I equalled with Ambani in wealth, I would fly from country to country and seek pleasures in every nook and corner of this globe.

She wishes she were equalled with Mother Teresa in care and compassion.

Though equally renowned in every street, the husband and the wife are poles apart at home.

Were the old useless lady equalled with Alexander in greatness, she would crow about her greatness all days and nights.

- **Reaping immortal faults of joy and love,**

Uninterrupted joy, unrivalled love,
In blissful solitude. ....

(Life has not given anyone on the earth guarantees and warranties, but every man expects life to be most joyous. Man expects joy to be uninterrupted without knowing the simple fact that mere joy does not teach him valuable lessons in life. The value of joy can be much felt in the presence of sorrow. The power of love remains unfelt as long as it remains unrivalled. To reap immortal joy, man reaps immortal faults without knowing that he will have to face the music on the Day of Judgment. When man is blessed with uninterrupted joy for years and years, he praises the Lord, but blames God, when his joy gets interrupted even for minutes. Is Man ungrateful to God? Is it the impact of every Man's first mother, who ate the fruit against the command of God who had blessed her with all extreme joys in paradise without expecting anything in return and without any need for anything in return?)

By sowing immortal faults, you are going to reap them one day or other.

I would like to have uninterrupted joy, whether I am in a club for excitement or an emergency ward.

Naveen can have uninterrupted joy, as long as his joy is interrupted by his wife.

Even though Ann has many rivals, her love with Antony remains unrivalled.

What bliss is needed in solitude? Many of us seek blessings in blissful solitude.

Toru wishes to remain a bachelor as he is of the strong belief that peace can be had only in blissful solitude.

The little boy tells her parents that he wants to study in a nursery school where his joy is uninterrupted, and love unrivalled.

- ....**Man will hearken to his glozing lies,**

  And easily transgress the sole command,
  Sole pledge of his obedience; so will fall
  He and his faithless progeny. Whose fault?
  Whose but his own?
  (Man will listen to his deceitful lies and readily offend against that one commandment which is the single guarantee of his

obedience. Thus man and his unfaithful posterity will fall.)

Speaking lies is more harmful than drinking and committing adultery. One lie leads to another. Mahatma Gandhi stood for 'Truth', so must be his followers. What benefits does one have in speaking lies? But it is said that a marriage could be performed even by speaking thousand lies, but arranging the marriage of a married man with the single lie that 'he is a bachelor' has its own consequences in families. One can live today because of a lie, but one day or other he/she will fall when Truth comes to light. Trust is tested because of lies. When a husband tells his wife that she is the most beautiful angel in the world, the wife may be happy because of her husband having a great admiration for her beauty, but the husband may consider his own comment a lie, for there is no angel in this world. Does he indirectly mean to say that his wife might go to Heaven to live among angels? Or does he mean to say that an angel sent from Heaven has become his wife on earth? If lie makes one happy, can it be spoken? Can it be called a 'white lie.' After marriage, the young husband impresses his young wife, telling her that she is the very first girl to be seen by him. He speaks this lie pertinaciously, for the eyes never speak verbally. On many occasions, speaking lies becomes inevitable.)

Man falls for his own faults but blames all except himself.

People hearken to the glozing lies and incredible promises of the politician and fall once in five years economically, socially and even psychologically.

It is your loyal service to dishonesty that will result in the fall of your progeny.

Many of us these days reach heights of glory with glozing lies.

Man will hearken to the glozing lies of Satan and lose angels.

• ....I created all the Ethereal Powers

And Spirits, ...
(Angels and Spiritual Beings)

(The rodomontade speeches of some of us are most irritating. They would speak as if they had the divine powers to create all the Ethereal Powers and Spirits, but they might, as a matter of fact, be mewing like cats at home. Man could never become God, even if he created the ethereal powers and spirits, or grew upto or beyond the sky.)

The employees say that their boss behaves as if he created all the Ethereal Powers.

When the ball is in the court of the Great Creator of all the Ethereal Powers, how can I tell you how long I will live and what will happen to me after my death?

"Even the Ethereal Powers and spirits cannot change my fate", say feelingly the farmers.

The saint threatens the innocent villagers with the lie that it was he who created all the Ethereal Powers and Spirits.

The arrogant rich man is looking for alliance for his only son who should have been blessed by all the Ethereal Powers and Spirits.

- **Both what they judge and what they choose:**

(A number of culprits may be punished, but not and never a single person of honesty, justice and integrity. When any judgment goes wrong, common man loses trust in justice and honesty. Judgement must be given only on the basis of Truth and Honesty, and that is why making comments on any judgment is considered 'contempt of court.' We judge one by one's appearance, but God looks at one's heart. "Appearance is deceptive" is a proverb in English. All are not saints that go to church. One who neither knows how to choose nor knows how to Judge is unfit to a leader or an administrator. Failure to judge one correctly is the main reason for the increasing number of the inefficient in many a workplace. When even noises are considered voices, voice loses its meaning. What one chooses and what one judges must be correct and fair.)

What I choose may be wrong, but what I judge won't be.

The father said to his son, "You choose someone and you judge, but never rely upon my choice and judgment."

All your decisions are based upon the choices and the judgments of introverted persons.

There is a whale of difference between your choice and judgment.

Both what they judge and what they choose are wrong, but they make sermons on Perfection.

- ....they themselves ordained their fall.

(In Tamil, it is said "Sontha selavil sooniyam vaippathu." This means 'going to the dogs at own efforts' or 'inviting own troubles'. Many of us, by own words and deeds, ordain our own fall but later try to blame all creatures under the sun. Adam and Eve ordained their own fall by disobeying the command of God. Had they not tasted the fruit from the Tree of Knowledge, they and we too would not have lost Paradise. Though we lost Paradise, we gained Milton's Paradise Lost. In Shakespeare's tragedies, the fall of the mighty heroes is because of some major flaw. Macbeth had his fall because of Lady Macbeth's avariciousness and over-vaulting ambition. When we analyse the reasons for one's fall in life, generally it is because of one's greediness. The Bhagavat Gita values 'self-contentment' as the highest achievement.)

They themselves ordained their fall, but now they are looking for coats to find holes.

When he himself wishes to have his fall, there is no point in our thinking of his upcoming.

It was their fate that they had themselves ordained their fall.

Fall is fall, whether it is the fall of a devil or that of man or an angel.

Had they consulted their conscience and common sense, they might not have ordained their fall.

- **Self-tempted, self-depraved........**

(self-tempted and self-corrupted)

(The best way of overcoming temptations is simply to yield to them. There is no need for many of us to get tempted by others, for they are self-tempted. Temptation is the outcome of ambition and discontentment. One who is self-tempted and self-depraved cannot attain perpetual peace. One who does not fall a prey to temptations is at peace. However, one must feel tempted by someone's intellect.)

Self-tempted and self-depraved, Tarun lost many an opportunity that knocked at his door many times.

Even though the politician is self-tempted and self-depraved, he has and follows certain principles in life.

Kannan says that his son became self-tempted and self-depraved only after his falling into the company of some jokers and drunkards.

Neither his parents nor his teachers taught him how to get tempted and depraved.

Being self-tempted and self-depraved, his mind is always haunted by evil thoughts and evil plans.

- ....Man, therefore, shall find grace,

The other none. In mercy and justice both,
Through Heaven and Earth, so shall my glory excel;
But mercy, first and last shall brightest shine"

(All creatures under the sun need grace, but not all have it. Many women whose minds are chained with superstitious beliefs lose peace of mind in their search for grace. The believers are prepared to suffer a lot in this world in order to enjoy perpetual grace in the next world. Is it Mercy that one brings one Grace? Or is it Grace that makes one merciful?)

Man seeking grace fall a prey in the hands of the so-called saints on many occasions.

Man cannot find grace till he finds himself.

"Justice cannot be expected in the absence of mercy, as I have neither proof nor any lawyer with me to prove my honesty in this case", says the poor man.

So arrogant Kevathi is that she behaves as if her glory had excelled through Heaven and Earth despite her being an absolute zero both personally and intellectually.

Those who are not gracious are looking for grace. Grace is not available in any place of worship, but in human heart, if it is in the right place.

Mercy, will you not shower upon me your brightest rays!

- **Beyond compare the Son of God was seen**

Most glorious: in him all his Father shone
Substantially expressed; and in his face
Divine compassion visibly appeared.
Love without end, and without measure grace;

(The Son of God appeared glorious beyond all comparison; in his person the nature of his Father was exhibited in substance; in his face divine compassion visibly appeared, and with its endless love and grace immeasurable.)

(Every child's face is shining with divine compassion, but it is visible to the eyes of those who have love and concern for children. Is there love without end? God's love has no end. There are many Romeos whose love ends when their Juliets look old. Ring is considered the token of love on marriage occasions, as ring has no end as love has no end. God did not beget any nor was He begotten, but human beings are called sons and daughters of God. Is it because of the endless love and immeasurable grace that God has bestowed upon all of us? It is also said that the pious people look most gracious and their faces shine with Divine compassion. They are the most blessed. They may suffer in this world, but they shall not be forgiven. They may lose piece of mind, but they have their own places in the Heart of God. They may lose everything in this world, but not God's endless love and immeasurable grace.)

He is No: 1 Satan but he says that divine compassion visibly appears in his face.

You cannot make divine compassion appear in your face just by washing your face with some 'face wash'.

My father and mother have for me love without end, and grace without measure.

Tom says that his wife tortures him with endless love and grace.

You can be most glorious but you cannot become God, for He is more gracious than the most gracious.

- **Or proud return, though to his heavier doom,**

**Yet with revenge accomplished, and to Hell
Draw after him the whole race of mankind,
By him corrupted?**

(The entire race of mankind got corrupted by Satan. The entire race of mankind could have purified Satan's heart by not falling a prey to his evil plans. Eve could have sought God's advice before putting her trust in Satan? What made Satan more appealing to Eve than the Creator? Was the sixth sense of our first mother so numbed in her conversation with the evil-tongued Satan? Or is it the plan of the Creator that Eve must fall a prey to Satan's words? When Satan is blamed for corrupting the whole race of mankind, the whole race of mankind must be blamed for not trusting God, for not using the sixth sense, for not being able to distinguish between what is right and what is wrong.)

The teacher tells the student that his very presence on the campus will corrupt the whole race of the student community.

Satan's main willing task is to draw after him to Hell the whole race of mankind.

Satan with his highly polluted and corrupted mind and heart can easily corrupt and pollute any human mind.

Man might say on the Day of Judgment, "By him I got corrupted, and by him, I am thrown into Hell. But the fire in the Hell may burn me, but not my sins."

When a country considers revenge a mark of accomplishment, war is the outcome.

The poor father says to his son, "For all my pains in bringing you up, the proud return can be your accomplishment in the field of education.

- **O Son, in whom my soul hath chief delight,**

Son of my bosom,...........................

(Prophet Muhammed Says, "Paradise lies at the feet of one's mother." The soul of one's mother's chief delight is in her own children. But are they affectionate towards their mother and father? Smart phones are closer to their hearts, and their parents have been kept far away. On one side, we take pride in the scientific and technological advancements, and on the other side, excessive use of technology has its own negative impact upon the younger generation. Many teenagers are technically sound but in the absence of care and compassion sine quo non for establishment and maintenance of human relations. They have time to play games in mobile phones, time to chat with friends, time to dine out, time to go for bike-race, time to sleep, but they have no time to spend even 10 minutes with their parents.)

They are my son and daughter in whom, having named them after my beloved parents, my soul hath chief delight.

We are all sons and daughters of God's bosom.

Once a son of the poor farmer's bosom, Anovan now wants his father to leave the house, unless the properties are registered in his name.

Your son who hates you now with his mind, heart and soul because of his blind love with the girl more cunning than a fox, worse than a devil, more poisonous than a snake, and hurts with with words most painful and unbearable, will one day attain maturity, realise the value of parental affection, come back to you as son of your bosom.

The girl, in whom the innocent boy hath chief delight, hath her chief delight in many other boys.

* ....once more I will renew

His lapsed powers, though forfeit and enthralled
By sin to foul exorbitant desires;

(Once again I will restore his fallen powers, though lost in consequence of his own fault and enslaved by sin to foul and immoderate desires.)

When Man easily and voluntarily falls a prey into the evil plans of Satan, is there any need that he must renew his lapsed powers. In stead of empowering himself with Divine Powers, it is the fate of Man that he is enthralled by sin. It is the over-vaulting ambition that makes Man commit sins. When Man's mind is filled with foul exorbitant desires, he loses his peace of mind. All his evil words and deeds renew the powers of Satan. Man is a tool in the hands of Satan, when God has him in His Heart. All is fair when Man is haunted by foul exorbitant desires.)

Innocent people are getting ready to renew the lapsed powers of their MLA, though he spent the entire five years in purchase of properties, expansion of families, opening of accounts in as many banks as possible.

Even if you are recharged and your powers are renewed, you will continue to behave like a fool.

Though forfeit and enthralled by sin to foul exorbitant desires, one can once more renew one's lapsed powers.

Though the old lady says that she has renewed herself, there is nothing new in her administration.

Though forfeit and enthralled by sin to foul exorbitant desires, Sanitha has not yet mended her evil attitude.

* ....I will clear their senses dark,

What may suffice, and soften stony hearts

To pray, repent, and bring obedience due,

(I will render their darkened senses clear as far as sufficient and soften their hearts of stone so that they may pray, repent and become obedient as they ought to be.)

Hearts cannot be softened as long as they are dark. Hearts cannot purified as long as Satan dwells there. Disobedience is the outcome of one's arrogance. Man invites troubles, when he disobeys the Creator and obeys the evil forces. He goes astray for he is not obedient to the Lord. Stony hearts cannot be softened unless the minds are clear. When the roots of mind get corrupted, there is no point in thinking of softening the hearts.)

He has no sense at all; how can you clear his senses dark? He has no heart at all; how can you say that his stony heart could be softened?

He may pray, but his prayed will not be accepted; he may repent, but his repentance will not have any immortal value and he may bring obedience, but obedience will lose its meaning.

Oh God! Clear my senses dark, soften my stony heart, fill my tongue with words in praise of you, let me pray and practise obedience to reach you with my flesh, heart and soul.

There are many saints but with senses dark, hearts but stony, faces but fake, but they pray, repent, pretend to bring obedience, but they do not know that their own organs will uncontrollably betray them on the Day of Resurrection.

- **Mine ear shall not be slow, mine eye not shut;**

(I will not be slow to hear....)

Man has two eyes and two ears but one tongue. So man must observe more; listen more and speak less. Ears, Minds and Eyes must be kept open. We have ears but we do not hear; we have eyes but we do not see; we have minds and hearts; but they are too dark to see the Light.)

The young girl says to her husband, "I am unable to utter a word. Your mother's ear is never slow, her eye never shut and she is vigilant days and nights. Whether walls have ears or not, your mother has ears and eyes open for me to keep me away from you.

The student tells his teacher that his ear is slow in his classes.

The old man says that his eyes are not shut, but he sleeps. His throat block his words, but he speaks.

Your ears are slow and your eyes are closed. How can you hear and see the world?

The boy says to his girl friend, "My ears are never slow to any of your words, even if you scold me or curse me.

- **And I will place within them as a guide**

My umpire Conscience, whom if they will hear,
Light after light, well used, they shall attain
And to the end persisting safe arrive
This my long sufferance and my dear of grace
They who neglect and scorn, shall never taste;
But hard be hardened, blind be blinded more,
That they may stumble on and deeper fall;

(Within their souls as a guide I will place conscience, my umpire which decides right and wrong; if they will listen to Conscience, they shall advance with enlightenment ever increasing in proportion as they use it well, and preserving to the end they shall reach the goal of Salvation. But this long endurance of mine and this my season of grace the neglectful and the scornful shall never experience; hard as they are they shall become still harder, and blind, still blinder that they may go stumbling onward and meet the deeper fall.)

(When temptations are more, does one consult one's common sense and conscience? Safe arrival might make one feel safe and secure, but does not one teach lessons most essential to understand life better. Man's intelligence is nothing before Divine Powers. When Man is destined to have his fall through Satan, and if it were the will of God, what could Man do? Man is a mini creature among elephant-like mammals. He is blind, but blinded more by temptations. Among all creatures, is Man the only creature endowed with all sorts of sufferings? Among all creatures, is Man the only creature destined to bear pain both physical and mental?)

Let conscience be your guide whenever your mind wavers due to temptations.

Even though there is light after light in life, Man with impatience and intolerance is in the dark.

Mercy is gracious to all her dear and near ones, but Grace is not dear to her.

The hard rules of the company will be hardened, if the blind are more blinded by the so-called benefits and profits available to them for the time-being.

You have a fall now, but beware of any deeper fall in future.

- **He with his whole posterity must die;**

(John Milton said, "Before I die, I wish to leave something which the posterity will not willingly let die." He has left with us his 'Paradise Lost', and made us regain our knowledge of the story of paradise lost. Adam and Eve might have lost Paradise, but the world of Literature got 'Paradise Lost' as a great treasure gained. The whole world with the whole posterity got Milton's literary works as most valuable treasures.

Even in extreme fury, any human being cannot curse anyone, saying 'He with his whole posterity must die.' For the faults of Tom, his grandsons cannot be punished. Such a sentence could be the outcome of one's uncontrollable anger. To the strong believers, man has no right to curse others, for any one-good or bad- is God's creature. It is also widely believed that those who curse others with no reason at all will have on their own heads the repercussions. So let us not curse anyone. One who controls his/her anger is greater than a great warrior in a battlefield. To dare is great, but to bear is greater.

Sevathy is such a cruel and heartless lady that she could pray that all on earth ,except her family, must die with their whole posterity.

If you say that she must die with her whole posterity, it shows the incurable pain she has given you.

None on earth can be cursed to suffer or die with his/her whole posterity.

All people on earth irrespective of religion, caste, colour and creed must live happily with their whole prosperity.

Let my friend who donated blood to all those in need, and lost his health must live with his children and grandchildren with extreme happiness and good health.

- ....death for death

('Dear for death' results in more deaths. Birth is the messenger of Death. Birth and Death are in the hands of the Lord. Man's brain is the greatest wonder in the world of Science and Technology. Man has been trying to make the moon the place to dwell in. He may even try to reduce the heat of the sun. He may even try to convert the days into nights and nights into days, but no man on the entire earth, however intelligent he/she is, can create a man or bring the dead back alive. Those who commit suicide shalt not enter the Heaven. Strict and barbaric adherence to the principle of 'Death for Death' poses a threat to peace and harmony for which the whole world and every creature on the earth has been craving for and struggling for and yearning for. 'Death for Death' is not a solution to Peaceful Life on earth. John F. Kennedy said, "Man must put an end to war or war will put an end to mankind.' Let us think of Birth, not of Death. However, when one, fearing death, leads a disciplined life following all ethical values and helping all, is honoured by Death, and Lives after Death under the shadow of the Creator.

One of the Tamil film directors K.Baagyaraj in his reply to one of the questions "How to get myself rid the fear of death?' raised by one of his readers replied: "Don't fear death. Death will not come to you as long as you are alive. When it comes to you, you will not be alive."

Life for life and Death for death.

The politician awards death even to those who gave him life when he was lifeless.

"'Death for death' is my policy", says the rowdy.

Birth and Death are in the Hands of the Lord. Birth is the Messenger of Death.

The poor father says to his arrogant son, "I gave you and all your plans life, but you have been planning to give me death."

• ....**where shall we find such love?**

(Everyone is in search of love in every nook and corner, when it is available at home. The love of mother is beyond comparison. Man goes to the street in search of love when it is not available at home. Some get it and many lose peace of mind. Mother-in-law becomes a mother, when her daughter-in-law enjoys her motherly love. Husband experiences motherly love even after his mother's death, if his wife's love is true. Father's love is as true as Mother's love, but generally father does not express his love, fearing the ill-effects of excessive love and freedom. God's love can be felt by the believers even in misfortunes. In many families, parents lose their peace of mind when their children go out in search of love. Shakespeare says in 'Merchant of Venice' that love is blind, and lovers cannot see the pretty follies that they themselves commit. Every lover promises that he will construct his own Taj Mahal for his own Mumtaz, whether he has even a penny in his purse or not. In giving promises, only the lovers can excel the politicians. Politicians win votes and lovers hearts, but both are experts in giving promises.

Adam and Eve lost the Divine love, when they fell into Satan's trap. Satan with his poisonous tongue pasted with love put an end to Divine Love. Man lost Paradise. Where shall we find Divine love on this earth?)

I say to my mother even after her death, "Oh my beloved mother! Where can I find such love as the love you bestowed on me every second you were alive?."

The boy says, "I find true love in everyone except the girl I am in love with."

Did Adam and Eve lose God's such love after disobeying His command?

The saint says, "I can find peace in my temple, love in God, but where can I find my bread?."

The parents say to their children, "When you find such love anywhere outside, come back home."

- **Comes unprevented, unimplored and unsought?**

(unanticipated, unimplored and unsought)

Everyone enjoys the true love of parents unprevented, unimpaired and unsought.

The poor man says, "After my wife's death, I was in search of my own children's love, but I did not get, though it was unprevented."

Love that comes unprevented, unimpaired and unsought is ignored by the romantic boy, whereas he is going after the arrogant girl like a mad dog, knowingly or knowingly that the girl has been a flower giving her evil fragrance to innumerable noses.

On many occasions, love given to us by unknown persons unprevented, unimpaired and unsought moves us to tears.

Love that come unprevented, unimpaired and unsought is true love.

- **.....................on me let Death wreak all his rage,**

**Under his gloomy power I shall not long
Lie vanquished; ....**

(Let death wreak all his fury on me. I shall not long be subject to his gloomy power.)

(What happens to one after death? Has anyone, after death, come back alive and shared his/her experiences with others? Does Death approach one as an Angel or as a Devil? Is one punished after Death? Does death embrace the dead with love or swallow them with rage? What are the ways in which the sinner are punished after their Death? What are the awards or rewards that the devotees are entitled to after Death? Can anyone describe the gloomy power of Death? Is there any Life after Death? Believers have their own answers to these questions, and non-believers too have their own answers. But as a matter of fact, only the Creator has answers to all these questions. However, non-believers are of the belief that there is no life after death. With death, comes to an end one's life.)

Tom is living under the gloomy power of Death.

How long can one live a life of peace and harmony under the gloomy power of Death?

Death can wreak all his rage on anyone at any time.

Under the gloomy power of Death, who will not long lie vanquished?

Death spreads its last bed before it approaches.

- **All that of me can die. Yet, that debt paid,**

  Thou wilt not leave me in the loathsome grave,
  His prey, nor suffer my unspotted soul
  For ever with corruption there to dwell;
  But I shall rise victorious, and subdue

(I am subject to death, yet once the debt is paid, you will not leave me in the horrible grave nor suffer my pure soul to rest for ever mingled with corruption. I shall rise victorious and subdue my conqueror.)

Lina was living like princess as long as he was his father's beloved daughter, but after marriage, her husband left her in the loathsome grave. Had her father come to know of this, even after death, he would have left himself in the loathsome grave.

All may love in this world but all will leave us in the loathsome grave.

None on earth accompanies or wishes to accompany one to the grave.

You may have a glorious path but it will lead to grave one day or other.

Better to suffer, suffocate and die out of hunger with a clear conscience and pure mind and heart than to dwell with corruption and contaminated mind and heart.

Sevathy will pay her debt for all her sins after her death. She can never rise happy or victorious, for God is always just.

- **Death his death's wound shall then receive........**

When many of us have experienced the pain of Life's wounds, why should we think of those of Death?

The girl says that she does not wish to receive again the wounds that she had had in the years gone.

Even while living, many old people receive death's wounds before they reach their last bed.

The arrogant old lady won't learn any lesson even from her death's wounds.

Better to receive death's wounds than to bear life's pains.

- **............to see thy face, wherein no cloud**

Of anger shall remain, but peace assured
And reconcilement; wrath shall be no more
Thenceforth, but in thy presence joy entire."

(After my long absence and return to see your face, on which no trace of anger shall remain but signs of lasting peace and reconciliation: thenceforward wrath shall cease and perfect joy only exists in your presence.)

We find clouds of anger on his face, when his father gave him some good advice.

Tom says to his son, "Your smile has vanished, and anger remains, and so has vanished your joy and so remains sorrow in your mind and heart."

Currency notes and all luxuries cannot assure peace of mind.

Wrath became no more after reconcilement between husband and wife.

The entire divine joy being experienced by Adam and Eve got lost like a river in the desert after the very presence of Satan.

- **And by thyself Man among men on earth**

The boys who destroyed the life of innocent young girls in Pollachi must be animals among men on earth.

He is a super man among men on earth.

Mere saintly look of yours does not make you a man among men on earth.

The girl asks her father whether he could not find for her some boy among boys on earth.

I am myself a man among men on earth. If you make me a Saint among men, I am not responsible for that.

- **His crime makes guilty all his sons;**

(Can anyone live in this world without committing crimes or sins? Why does Man become a sinner, despite all teachings and preachings? Has Man not yet learnt lessons from the lives of the sinners in the previous years? Is Man not aware of the consequences of facing the Creator as a sinner in this world on the Day of Resurrection? A father's crime makes all his sons guilty. A son's crimes makes his father feel ashamed. One cannot carry with him/her to his/her grave someone's sins. On the Day of Judgment, one is answerable to God for someone else's sins. However, parents, who fail to execute their duties as responsible parents, are answerable to God on the Day of Judgment. In our society, when someone goes wrong or indulges in crimes, the society blames the parents.)

One cannot be punished for someone's crime.

One person cannot vomit for another person's nausea.

The crime of a father makes his heir guilty.

The party leader's crime makes guilty all party men.

Some of us commit crimes many times, but we never feel guilty even once.

- **.............both righteous and unrighteous deeds,**

(There can be none on earth without both righteous and unrighteous deeds. But the unrighteous deeds must turn out to be righteous ones. As long as Satan haunts one's mind, nothing can be right. What is totally wrong will appear to be totally correct. Self-realisation is important. One must scan one's own life. According to Plato, life not self-examined is not life worth living. On the Day of Judgment, Man is answerable to God for both all his righteous and unrighteous deeds. No man can escape, projecting himself with only righteous deeds and hiding all his unrighteous ones, for God is omniscient.)

Some are righteous in words but unrighteous in deeds.

Man is noted for both righteous and unrighteous deeds.

When Man is awarded and rewarded for unrighteous deeds and blamed and cornered for righteous deeds, right and wrong cannot be distinguished.

The politician says that he will be noted for righteous deeds at the time of election and for the unrighteous deeds after the election.

Man is answerable to God on the Day of Resurrection both for his righteous and unrighteous deeds. If Man's life is unrighteously noted for righteous deeds, he will be righteously punished for the unrighteous life.

- **Receive new life. ....**

The boy tells his new wife that he feels a new life being lived after marriage.

The old parents have received new life after being forsaken by their children in life.

I have received new life by writing books and by sharing knowledge with others.

If Adam and Eve had not fallen a prey to satan's evil plans, every day of their life in Paradise would have made them enjoy the feeling of a new life received.

The young mother says that she has received a new life after the birth of his beloved son.

Whether you receive new life or not, you renew and reform and refine your present life.

He thought that he would receive a new life after his marriage, but he lost his entire life as Adam and Eve lost their Paradise.

- **So heavenly love shall outdo hellish hate,**

(God's love shall defeat the malice of Hell.)

Satan fills the hell with his hellish love.

Heavenly love shall outdo hellish hate, but when can hell be destroyed?

Fill our hearts with heavenly love.

James is looking at his father with hellish hate in his mind and heart.

When you believe that heavenly love shall outdo hellish hate, why should you continue to fall a prey to the evil words of devils around you?.

- **............................throned in highest bliss,**

Equal to God, and equally enjoying
Godlike fruition, ...

(.........enthroned in supreme happiness as equal of God and capable of perfect enjoyment equally with Him.....)

Though enthroned in highest bliss, many of us do not have the 'contentment'.

Many of us are so avaricious that they foolishly love to find themselves equal to God.

If Adam and Even had not tasted the fruit from the Tree of Knowledge, they could have been equally enjoying Godlike fruition.

What is the use of wishing to be throned in highest bliss without peace of mind?

With all inventions in science and technology, Man can never become equal to God.

- ....to save

A world from utter loss; hast been found
By merit more than birthright Son of God,
Found worthiest to be so by being good,
Far more than great or high; because in thee
Love hath abounded more than glory abounds;

(............to save a world from absolute destruction, and since thou hast been proved the Son of God by merit, not by mere hereditary claim, being shown to be most deserving of that name by the goodness far more than by thy greatness or dignity, and since thy love has exceeded thy glory...........)

The world cannot be saved from utter loss without God's mercy.

The boy said the principal that he had to be given admission by the birthright son of the college secretary rather than by merit.

The saint claims himself to be the birthright Son of God and therefore the govt has taken back from all his rights as citizen of the nation.

The poor boy, though found worthiest, was rejected by the worthless interviewers.

July loves joes as she finds in him both love and glory in abundance.

- **The World shall burn, and from her ashes spring**

New heaven and earth, wherein the just shall dwell,
(Faith is beyond one's logical thinking, or any logical reason. This world, to the faithful, is like a prison and they do not trust

this world. They do believe that there is going to be another new world after death. There is going to be an 'extremely happiest and immortal life in Paradise' for one who had lived an honest life, fearing the Creator.)

When will happiness spring in my life?

If only the just live in the world, there may not be any genuine reason for the world to burn.

The world shall burn, and from her ashes new heaven and earth, but if man is burned, nothing comes from his ashes.

The saint says that he is waiting for the world wherein the just shall dwell.

From all ashes, heaven and earth cannot be expected to spring.

- ....Omnipotent

Immutable, Immortal, Infinite,
Eternal King; Author of all being,
Fountain of light, thyself invisible
(....all powerful, unchangeable, undying........the source of light)

Don't talk so arrogantly as though you were born omnipotent, omnipresent and omniscient.

Man's life is not infinite and so must at least be his love for the fellow human beings.

Sevathy speaks as if she were the fountain of light but her behaviour darkens the minds of all around her.

If I were invisible, I would not leave the corrupt and the dishonest officers freely.

You may be an eternal king but your life is not eternal.

He is not aware of his own 'being' but says that he is the author of all being.

Only God is omnipotent, omnipresent, omniscience, Eternal King, Gracious Lord, Immutable, immortal, Infinite and the real Author of all creatures.

- **To execute fierce vengeance on his foes.**

Her only hobby is to execute fierce vengeance on his foes.

By executing fierce vengeance on all others, do you think that you can lead a peaceful life?

The best way of executing fierce vengeance on your foes is to painfully forgive them, to happily chat with them and to make them friends.

By executing fierce vengeance on his foes, what he has earned in life is mere enmity.

Without foes, the mad fellow has executed fierce vengeance on himself.

- **Father of mercy and grace, ...**

(A nurse is called a 'sister of mercy'.)

Tom says that David is his father but not of mercy and grace.

Is it because of God being the Father of extreme mercy and grace, the number of sinners is rapidly increasing?

With no mercy and grace in mind and heart, we seek God's mercy and grace.

She says that though his father is not rich, he is more than the Father of mercy and grace in being merciful and gracious.

"Our boss is Father of mercy and grace", say the employees.

- **...................................O, unexampled love!**

Love nowhere to be found less than Divine!
Hail, Son of God, Saviour of men! Thy name
Shall be the copious matter of my song

(...love without example, love Divine, and nothing less, in nature! ....Thy name shall be an ample theme for my song.)

Nikitha's love towards Ratan is unexampled and divine.

The Saint says that he is the son of God, but whatever he speaks and does creates doubts whether he is the son of God or the most affectionate and most loyal devotee of Satan.

Peter says, "My love is nowhere to be found less than Divine, but no one is prepared to love me."

The poet tells his girl friend that her beauty shall be the copious matter of his entire poetry.

(Boy: My love for you is divine and unexampled.

Girl: Every lover says that his love is divine, but how can I believe that it is unexampled?

Boy: Ask your sister how I loved her. That is the best example.

Girl: !!!)

- **Dark, waste, and wild, under the frown of Night**

   Starless exposed, and ever-threatening storms
   Of Chaos blustering round, inclement sky,

(....dark, desolate and wild, lying open and starless under the lowering Night, with ever-threatening storms of chaos blustering round, the whole presenting a sky.....)

(Student: How can I sail in ever-threatening storms, Sir?

Teacher: Storm, lightening and thunder will teach you more valuable lessons than roses in your life journey.)

The girl says that she never imagined that her life after marriage would become dark, waste, and wild, under the frown of night starless exposed, and, ever-threatening storms of chaos blustering round, inclement sky.

The poor farmers say, "Our sky is starless, our days and nights are lifeless, our days are dark, our lives are waste, and we have ever-threatening storms though there are no signs of rain."

Nights can be starless but life should not be lifeless.

There may be threatening thunders, but I won't be afraid of sailing.

- **Living or lifeless, ...**

(Life not examined is not life worth living.- Plato)

If a researcher does not give life to his/her thoughts , research is lifeless.

After living for more than 98 years, Sevathy, at her eleventh hour, says that her life was totally lifeless as she could not take revenge upon some of her rivals.

Living or lifeless, one must be happy and healthy.

The poor parents deserted by selfish children are living but their life is lifeless.

When every second of yours is lifeless, how can you say that you are living?

- **Built their fond hopes of glory or lasting fame,**

 Or happiness in this or the other life.

I am building my fond hopes, hoping against hope.

There may be happiness but not in the life she is leading now.

Losing the life being led, one cannot borrow life from any, seeking happiness.

With hopes of glory, the lazy fellow is wasting time from sunrise to sunset.

I wish you reached heights of glory and lasting fame.

- **The Paradise of Fools;....................**

"Better to suffer with devil in Hell than to enjoy life in the Paradise of Fools", says Ravivarman.

Fools are fools, whether they are in Paradise or Hell.

The politician says that he will learn evil ways of living from the devils of Hell instead of having pleasures from the Paradise of Fools.

The poor girl says, "I am prepared to be a fool in Paradise but I can no more live in this advancing world of science and technology without a piece of bread for my burning stomach."

The whole gang permanently dwells in the Paradise of Fools.

- **The work as of a kingly palace-gate,**

With frontispiece of diamond and gold
Embellished; thick with sparkling orient gems

(The work of a royal palace gate, made beautiful with front of diamond and gold; thick with sparkling lustrous gems the gateway shone-no model on Earth, no picture by shading brush could imitate it.)

The pauper imagines the work as of a kingly palace-gate with frontispiece of diamond and gold embellished; thick with sparkling orient gems.

The boy says that if she gives him her consent to marry him, he will build a house for her with all gates, windows and walls with diamond and gold.

The house has been constructed with gold and diamond stones imported from many countries but the house owner and his wife have neither a heart nor a mind to help any.

The bride has bought a sari thick with sparkling orient gems.

"Neither your gold car nor your diamond ornaments will make you live in the hearts of the people but your services", say the people to their MP.

- **Dreaming by night under the open sky,**

And waking cried, This is the gate of Heaven.

Many sinners of the first water are dreaming day and night of getting closer to the gate of Heaven without knowing that the Hell is ready to swallow them.

The poor people say that they can see the gate of Heaven while sleeping under the open sky every night but the rich can see only the walls of the rooms, though fully air-conditioned.

Dreams by night under the open sky one day or other might turn out to be a reality of the day.

Heaven may have gates but will they be kept open for all?

Sinners cannot become Saint when they go close to the gate of Heaven.

• ....whether to dare

The fiend by easy ascent, or aggravate
His sad exclusion from the doors of bliss;
(.....either to tempt the Fiend by the easy ascent they offered or to make his sad exclusion from Heaven still more grievous to bear.)

Man has no right to exclude anyone from the doors of bliss, but only God can do so.

His only hobby is to dare his every fiend by easy ascent without knowing that he will have his exclusion from the doors of bliss.

The doors of bliss are not made with currency notes.

The house filled with love has the doors of bliss.

• **Like those Hesperian Gardens famed of old,**

(They seemed like other worlds or like happy isles such as those Hesperian Gardens renowned in olden time.)

Even though those people have been living in abject penury for years and years, they feel like living at Hesperian Gardens.

If you think that you can have happiness only at Hesperian Gardens, you will lose your happiness and peace of mind.

My friend has constructed a beautiful bungalow with all facilities reminding anyone of the Buckingham Palace and the Hesperian Gardens.

This bee wants honey sucked from the flowers of Hesperian Gardens famed of old.

The bride considers the bridegroom a 'boomer uncle' as he wishes to go to Hesperian Gardens famed of old.

• **The place he found beyond expression bright,**

Compared with aught on Earth, metal or stone-
(He found the place bright beyond all description in comparison with anything on Earth, whether metal or stone.)

The hall is bright beyond expression.

His cabin is bright beyond expression but his mind is dark.

During the princess's wedding, every hall even at nights was beyond expression bright, compared with aught on earth, metal or stone.

He is such a close-eyed and narrow minded person that he would not care to see anything, even if he were to live in a place beyond expression bright, compared with aught on earth, metal or stone.

There is no point in your house being bright but it is your heart and mind that must be bright with good thoughts.

- **Philosophers in vain so long have sought;**
- Dr Albert is a philosopher in vain but he is much sought after by all researchers.

Though a philosopher in vain, he speaks only philosophy.

His association with philosophers in vain has finally made him a great philosopher.

Even philosophers in vain have started speaking of philosophy.

Some philosopher in vain has adjudicated Tom's thesis.

- **................................yet such as in his face**

Youth smiled celestial and to every limb
Suitable grace diffused; ....
(yet still such that celestial youth beamed in his face and shed a fitting grace upon his limbs.)

Though you are old, youth smiles in your face.

I do not find her face fit for smile or grace.

Smile smiles at your face and Grace is gracious to you.

Smile lost its smile the very moment you showed your face to smile.

The sun smiles at every one in early mornings but during hot summer, its smile troubles all.

- **The Archangel Uriel, one of the seven**

Who in God's presence nearest to his throne,
Stand ready at command

(The flatterers and the good-for-nothing persons are always willing to stand ready at the command of their boss and bow before them any number of times. Wise men try to impress their boss with their works, but the useless people do with their words of flattery. If an arrogant person comes to power, he/she might expect even the Archangel Uriel to stand outside their window ready at command. Even the archangel Uriel cannot be expected to have a thorough knowledge, just because of Uriel's nearest presence to His throne.)

There is nothing in your desire to go near to God's throne, but do not go away from human beings.

She makes commands as if she were the Archangel Uriel.

I said to parents, "I always stand ready at your command.'

The Archangel Uriel can be near to God's throne but cannot become God.

How long can I stand at your command?

- **Unspeakable desire to see and know**

All these his wonderous works, but chiefly Man.

(Man does wonders, but creation of man itself is a wonder. When we visit many countries and meet people, when we visit jungles and see animals and birds, when we see Nature, we develop unspeakable desire to see more and know more. Researchers must have unspeakable desire to see and know. There won't be any invention without the desire to see and know. A woman carrying her baby in the womb has unspeakable desire to see and know her baby. A father has unspeakable desire to see and know the prosperous growth of his children. Grandparents have unspeakable desire to play with their grandchildren. God has unspeakable desire to find Man grateful and good, loving and helping, considerate and compassionate. A good teacher must have unspeakable desire to learn more and more and to share more and more. Politicians should have unspeakable desire to serve the people, but should not have the unspeakable desire to open accounts in all banks of Swiss. When politicians have unspeakable desire to wallow in wealth, people must have unspeakable desire to punish them at the time of election through their votes. God had and has the unspeakable desire to create Man as His best piece of art, but the envious Satan with unspeakable desire to turn against the Creator has been spoiling man's mind in a number of ways.)

Every Romeo is burning with unspeakable desire to win his Juliet.

Man created in His image is God's wondrous work.

Man has become more ungrateful to the Creator than Satan who makes man ungrateful.

With an unspeakable desire to see the world and know of it more and more, my uncle is flying from country to country.

The innocent daughter-in-law has been experiencing unspeakable troubles and tortures since she got married in 1999.

- **For neither man nor angel can discern**

Hypocrisy- ....

(Hypocrisy is more harmful than enmity. Even a person with his/her heart in the right place can be or can turn out to be one's enemy, but no good person can be a hypocrite. All religions insist on one not being a hypocrite. The world has paid the heaviest price because of hypocrisy. Hypocrisy covers one's face, mind and heart with dark clouds. Hypocrisy cannot be and can never be the characteristic of any angel, or any with hypocrisy cannot be an angel. Man's downfall lies in hypocrisy. Muslims use the word 'Munafic' to mean a hypocrite. An enemy can be trusted with a secret, but certainly not a hypocrite. The tongue of a hypocrite has words but meanings are unknown or hidden. The heart of a hypocrite beats but for an evil cause. The mind of a hypocrite works but adversely and dangerously. Neither man nor angel can discern hypocrisy. Angels cannot discern hypocrisy, but man?)

What can be discerned by Satan cannot be discerned either by man or by angel.

Whether angel can discern hypocrisy or not, many men and women these days are able to discern hypocrisy.

When man capacitates himself to discern hypocrisy, he finds out the true colour of Satan.

There is no need for an angel to discern hypocrisy.

At the time of elections, people must be made able to discern hypocrisy.

• ....Suspicion sleeps

At Wisdom's gate, ...
(Whether suspicion sleeps at wisdom's gate or not, suspicion does not allow one to enjoy a sound sleep. A girl might accept a drunkard as a life partner, but not a doubting Thomas- a person with a suspicious mind. If a husband is a doubting Thomas, his wife is sure to lose her peace of mind.)

Unless the suspicion of Roger dies, he cannot lead a peaceful life with his wife.

It is most unfortunate knowledge and wisdom knock at the doors of Luck, seeking its grace on many occasions these days.

Peace is awake when suspicion sleeps.

One cannot become wise just by sleeping or waiting at wisdom's gate.

The gate of wisdom is not open for fools.

CHAPTER THREE

EXPRESSIONS AND EXPLANATIONS OF PART - IV

- ....warning voice, ...

The staff members feel that their Director addresses them in every meeting with a warning voice.

Though Minu is a baby, she has a warning voice.

You cannot control me with your warning voice, but with warm love.

Why is your voice so warning? Have some bone of bull got struck in your throat?

Because of her warning voice, there are many voices against her.

- ....our first parents had been warned

The coming of their secret foe, ...

The boy says to his parents, "How could you expect me to be obedient when the first parents themselves were not obedient to the Creator?".

Had the first parents been warned the coming of their secret foe, they would not have lost paradise.

Man must lose paradise. Perhaps that might have been the main reason why our first parents were not warned the coming of their secret foe.

Even after losing paradise, we have secret foes everywhere.

Secret foes do not do anything publicly.

- **Satan, now first inflamed with rage, came down,**

Whenever he shouts at me, I am reminded of Satan inflamed with rage when thrown out of Heaven.

There is nothing wrong in your being inflamed with rage, but you never come down.

Though inflamed with rage, the officer, understanding the situation, immediately came down.

Whenever she inflamed with rage shouts at her husband, the family members do not allow her to come down.

You become worse than Satan whenever you get inflamed with rage.

- **...................................Horror and doubt distract**

His troubled thoughts, ...
(Horror and doubt agitated his mind and thoughts.)
Horror and doubts distract and trouble his thoughts.
Distracted by horror and doubt and troubled by unwanted thoughts, the police officer shot himself down.
More than horror and doubt that distracted him, and more than thoughts that troubled him, it was, despite his efficiency and diligence, the stagnation in his position that made him go mad.
I am not a saint to send prayers to Heaven even when horror and doubt distract me and thoughts trouble me and failures disappoint me.

Horror has removed peace from his mind; doubt has distracted his concentration and thoughts have troubled his mind, but you expect him to work with more energy and spirit.

- **O sun, to tell thee how I hate thy beams,**

  That bring to my remembrance from what state
  I fell, how glorious once above thy sphere,
  Till pride and worse ambition threw me down,
  I hate the beams of the sun but I cannot be away from the sun.

  The anger of the sun is revealed through its beams!

  Pride and ambition threw not only Satan down, but also his followers.

  The minister who was glorious once lost everything because of his pride and ambition.

  Even though man knows that pride and ambition will throw him down, it is unknown why he loves to enjoy the so-called delights of pride, ambition, jealousy and discontentment.

  Had Adam and Eve not fallen a prey to pride and ambition, how glorious they would have been!

- ....I was

  In that bright eminence
  Roger is bright, but not his eminence in any way.

  His mind is dark, but his eminence is bright.

  It is your bright eminence that has elevated your position.

  Like Satan, the team leader is using his bright eminence to darken the brightness of eminence of the team members.

  David was in that bright eminence as long as his eminence was doubted and questioned by his own son.

- ....all his good proved ill in me,

  And wrought but malice.

(All his benefits turned out to produce a bad effect, and made me not grateful but malicious.)

Though all his good proved ill in Jenifer, she loves him more than she loves her own soul and life.

All the attempts put forth by the doctor proved ill in the patient.

When all your good proved ill in me, how could you expect me to trust you hereafter?

The farmers say that the govt has implemented all schemes in a malicious manner.

- ....Lifted up so high,

I disdained subjection, and thought one step higher
Would set me highest, and in a moment quit
The debt immense of endless gratitude,
So burdensome, still paying, still to owe; ....

(As he had placed me so high in Heaven, I started disdaining all subjection, and I thought that one step higher would place me at the highest position in Heaven. This thought made me oblivious of all the immense honours and benefits that God had conferred on me. Those favours being so immense that however I might have tried to pay them back, I was ever to remain indebted to Him.)

High position makes the greedy think always that they must be lifted up and up and that one step every day would set them highest.

The old fellow, even after retirement, desires to be lifted up higher than the heights at which eagles fly without thinking that a mighty fall one day or other for some reason or for no reason would totally damage his face.

He served the people for years and years and so they return in their own ways with endless gratitude.

The young boy was lifted up so high and set highest and so he has totally forgotten how to walk on the surface.

Many of us, being lifted up high, are invisible.

The affectionate son says that his father has become so burdensome that he would be prepared to say 'bye' to him any time.

Years ago Joe helped me once or twice, but I am still paying for that.

- ....love or hate,

To me alike it deals eternal woe.
Love and hate are alike to me.
The saint says that he considers love and hate alike. He adds that when he is loved by love, he shares it with others, and when he is loved by hate, he loves himself.
How long can I live with eternal woe?
By winning your love, you have fallen into eternal love.
Kabir considers love and hate alike as he lives with his mother and wife.

- ....the Hell I suffer seems a Heaven.

Whenever the Heaven I enjoy turns out to be or seems to be a Hell, it gives me immense pain.
The Hell I suffer seems a Heaven when my beloved daughter wipes my tears and worries with her words and smiles.
The farmers say that they continue to suffer whether the nation is a Hell or Heaven.
The newly married girl says that the only Hell she suffers day and night is her husband.
Even the Hell they suffered for years seems a Heaven, whenever they think of the horrible days under the old ghost.

- ....my dread of shame

Among the Spirits beneath, whom I seduced
With other promises and other vaunts
Than to submit, boasting I could subdue
The omnipotent. Ah me! They little know
How dearly I abide that boast so vain,

Under what torments inwardly I groan.

(If I surrender myself to God, I shall put myself to great shame before other fallen angels whom I persuaded to rebel against God with promises and assurances different from submission to him. I had boasted that I could subdue the Omnipotent God. Ah, woe for me, they do not know what a heavy penalty I have to pay for my vain boast and under what internal torments I groan.)

He was as incredible as a politician in his promises, as proud as a peacock, as boasting as a bridegroom's sister during wedding, as disobedient and arrogant as Satan, but none on earth can even imagine how dearly he abides those inhuman vices so vain, under what torments inwardly he groans.

One can feel ashamed of oneself among devils, but not among angels.

Even the devils are sure to feel ashamed of the inhuman, barbaric and animalistic attitude of the human-animals who ill-treated the fellow human beings in the name of race and caste in Manipur.

Some atheists find pleasure in boasting that they could subdue the omnipotent.

Man has to learn a lot of discipline from the crows but he just crows about his so-called accomplishments.

* ....wounds of deadly hate have pierced so deep-

Which would but lead me to a worse relapse

(It would bring over me heavier punishment.)

There is nothing in my heart and soul but the wounds of deadly hate that have pierced so deep.

All your arrogance, involvement in inhuman activities will lead you to a worse relapse.

When she gets angry, her every word is more deadly than the deadly poison.

I cannot count the number of wounds that have pierced me so deep.

My aim is not lead the culprits to a worse relapse but to direct them towards honesty and piety.

- **Mankind created, and for him this world!**

Man was created and for him was created this world.

Man was created, and to spoil him was created Satan.

God created Man not for him to boast of his being created but to praise the Lord for the creation.

Man remains ungrateful to the Creator till he is made to lie in his last bed.

Might the world have been created for all creatures except for Man?

- ....All good to me is lost;

Evil, be thou my good:
(Evil! Be by my side.)

The husband says, "Evil, you need not be by my side, for my wife is always by my side, reminding me of you."

All good to me is lost but I won't stoop down to the level of begging evil to be by my side.

There is nothing good in you to get lost and so there is no need for any devil to be by your side.

The silence of the govt over the inhuman incidents in Manipur might make the innocent women there say "Evil, be thou my good."

The students say to their teacher, "Sir, be thou our evil, but not our teacher."

- ....while he spake, each passion dimmed his face,

Thrice changed with pale-ire, envy, and despair;
(Satan's face became pale under the influence of anger, envy and despair.)

Anger, envy, ego, enmity, despair, revenge, jealousy and all other vices have further dimmed Sevathy's face.

When you speak, we feel the reflections of joy on your face.

She is so full of mixed passions that each passion dims her face.

The actress has no passion of any kind, for she does not like to have her face dimmed by any passion.

How can you think of seeking God's blessings as long as you are under the influence of all the vices under the sun?

- ....**was the first**

That practised falsehood under saintly show,

(Man looks at one's face, but God at one's heart. Man may judge a book by its cover but God knows every word of everyone's book (Life). None on earth can cheat the Creator by practising falsehood under saintly show. Man thinks that he can enter Heaven just by entering the place of worship, but God's will is that Heaven must have Man whose heart beats for the poor and yearns for offering services. Service to humanity is service to God. Honest and straightforward people never practise falsehood and there is no need for them to practise falsehood.)

The are many fake saints practising falsehood under saintly show.

Practising falsehood, you are acting as if you were the most purified soul.

"There is nothing wrong in practising falsehood, but not under saintly show", said the people to the saint.

The politician is an expert in practising falsehood under saintly show.

Falsehood is perfectly staged mostly under saintly show.

- **Shade above shade, ...**

(trees appearing one over the other)

I have a beautiful garden where there are shades and above shades.

The politician cut all the trees on his way and prevented people to relax under any shadow, but there is not even a single tree in his grave yard to give him shade.

The forest is so thick with trees in thousands that none can see the sun from inside. There is shade above shade.

After hard labour, the farmers are relaxing a little under shade above shade.

Shade above shade, but is hot his mind.

- ....to the heart inspires

Vernal delight add joy, able to drive
All sadness
Alas! Will not sadness drive all my sadness!
Man thinks that money can drive all his sadness.
Vernal delight adds joy to his mind and heart.
Unless there is joy in heart, will there be joy in mind?
He under the impact of some devil added joy to joy, further added joy to joy, and finally overjoy landed him in all sorrows.

- ....who sail

Beyond the Cape of Hope
(beyond the Cape of Good Hope)
There may be some hope even beyond the Cape of hope.
He wishes to sail amidst waves, as he predicts some hope beyond the Cape of Hope.
Losing hopes that she has, she is sailing beyond the Cape of Hope.
After losing all your hope, why should you think of sailing beyond the Cape of Hope?
Let me sail beyond the Cape of Hope, hoping that there will be some hope.

- ....As when a prowling wolf

Whom hunger drives to seek new haunt for prey,
(A cunning wolf driven by hunger seeks new haunts of prey.)
The young boy is looking at the beautiful girl like a prowling wolf.

When hunger drives to seek new haunt for prey, Irfan becomes a prowling wolf.

How can the girls be safe when they are surrounded by prowling wolves.

David says, "I can feed the hungry humans, but not prowling wolves."

Some poor parents struggle a lot to protect their beautiful daughters from prowling wolves roaming about with political influence.

- **Out of the fertile ground he caused to grow**

All trees of noblest kind for sight, smell, taste;
I wish to have all trees of noblest kind for sight, smell, taste in my garden.

Even the trees of noblest kind for sight, smell and taste could not satisfy Eve. She wanted to have her shade under some other tree and lost all trees.

There were all trees of noblest kind for sight, smell and taste, but not for senses.

Just because you enjoy the shades under the trees of noblest kind for sight, you cannot become a person of nobility.

Such a skilled farmer he is that he, out of the fertile ground, caused to grow all trees of noblest kind for sight, smell and taste.

- **Our death, the Tree of Knowledge, grew fast by-**

Knowledge of good bought dear by knowing ill.

(Tree of Knowledge brought the knowledge of Good along with the knowledge of evil.)

Should Man face his fate by tasting a fruit, that too, from the Tree of Knowledge?

Had Eve had a sound knowledge of the Tree of Knowledge, she might not have lost her knowledge and the Paradise as well.

He knows well all the ills of the life that he has been leading.

By knowing ill, one is not going to become a devil.

- **Flowers of all hue, and without thorn the rose.**

You can find flowers of all hue in our garden.

This bee is fond of flowers of all hue.

Tom says that his girl friend is a rose without thorn.

George says to Rohit, "If you go after my rose, I will be the thorn."

You have flowers of all hue, and you choose your rose now.

- ....all kind

Of living creatures, new to sight and strange.

His appearance is new to our eyes and so strange it is.

He said to his friend, "I found all kinds of living creatures in the zoo, except you."

Are all kind of living creatures grateful to the Creator?

What you say is quite strange to my ears.

Last night I saw in the sky a star new to sight and strange.

- **In naked majesty seemed lords of all;**

And worthy seemed; for in their looks divine
The image of their glorious Maker shone,
Truth, wisdom, sanctitude severe and pure-
Severe, but in true filial freedom placed,
Where true authority in men: though both

Not equal, as their sex not equal seemed:
For contemplation he and valour formed,
For softness she and sweet attractive grace;
He for God only, she for God in him.

(They were naked, clad only in pure native honour, in which they appeared divinely majestic. They appeared to be the lords of this new world, worthy and honourable. Their countenances clearly revealed that they had been made in God's own image. God endowed with divine virtues like truth, wisdom and holiness-pure and severe, with true paternal love and freedom of will allowed to children, and it was from this fact that they held their authority over all birds and beasts of Paradise. But for themselves they were not equal and their sex was not the same. Man was specially designed for independent thinking and heroic deeds, and woman for soft elegance and sweet attractive grace. Man is the image and glory of God and none else, but woman is the image and glory of man who is her God.)

Do not be naked in your use of language.

Equality is not needed only in sex but also in status, position, power and wealth.

I found the image of the glorious Maker shining on his face at his death bed. It may be because of the pure and perfect life that he had led on this earth as a dedicated teacher and as a good fellow human being.

He may look majestic in his walk and talk but all know pretty well that his majesty is naked and so his honour.

- ....banished from man's life his happiest life.

You can banish from my life anything but not my happiness.

When God banishes happiness from one's life, it need not be taken as a curse on him/her.

The old lady is leading her life with all diseases, after intentionally banishing from everyone's life happiness.

To favour people of his faith, the brutal beast of the earth banished happiness from the life of all those who had different faiths.

After marriage, the arrogant girl banished happiness and joy from the life of her husband and mother-in-law and father-in-law.

- ....the loveliest pair

That ever since in love's embraces met:
Adam the goodliest man of men since born
His sons, the fairest of her daughters Eve.
(the loveliest pair since seen in purest love. Adam was the most handsome of man's sons, and Eve the most beautiful daughter.)

The goodliest man of all men of the earth wishes to marry the fairest of all girls.

The Eve of his family is looking for a suitable Adam, matching her in every aspect.

The lovers embrace without their love embracing them.

David says to his daughter, "If you keep on waiting for the goodliest man of men, you will remain unmarried till the end of your life."

If everyone wishes to marry the fairest daughter, we will have to import parents from heaven.

- **All beasts of the earth, ...**

The beasts of Manipur paraded the innocent woman naked during the unpleasant situation there.

All beasts of the earth have formed an association to dislodge their common rivals.

All beasts of the earth are delivering lectures on peace and harmony.

Daniel tells his son that he has friendship with all beasts of the earth.

You are a beast not in appearance but in characteristics.

- ....the unwidely elephant

(the huge elephant)

The father-in-law says to his son-in-law, a house husband, "I cannot feed an unwidely elephant every day.

Lekha says to her husband, "How can I live with you when you behave like an unwidely elephant?."

When you are too weak to bear the bite of a mosquito, you desire to be crushed by an unwidely elephant.

Whenever there is a fight between the mother-in-law and the daughter-in-law, the neighbours are reminded of the aggressive fight between two unwidely elephants in a thick forest.

We do not know how the lean funny, puny, little creature gave her consent to marry such an unwidely elephant.

- ....when all these delights

Will vanish, and deliver ye to woe-
More woe the more your taste is now of joy;
Happy, but for so happy ill secured
Long to continue, ...

(All these delights will very soon vanish, and you will fall to grief, and your grief will be proportionate to the amount of happiness lost. You are so happy, but for this great happiness you are not sufficiently secured to preserve this happiness for long.)

Man is yearning for more and more delights, and more delights give him more woe.

Man is contented to remain as a saint when all his delights vanish.

Man longs to be happy and expects his happiness to remain for long.

None on earth tried to think over his/her eligibility to enjoy happiness.

As Man thinks of God in woe and of Satan in happiness, he loses happiness and stays with woe after his 'life exam on earth' is over.

- **"Sole partner and sole part of all these joys**

Tom married her in the hope that she would be throughout his life the sole partner and sole part of all his joys without knowing his entire life would be full of sorrows.

How can one tolerate the pain caused by the sole partner and sole part of one's whole life?

He considered his son his sole part of all his joys but he made his father's life most sorrowful by shouting at him, by ignoring him, by disrespecting him and by making him a solitary reaper at his old age.

The old man says, "Oh God! Make myself sole part of my own joys.

He says that his wife is his sole partner and sole part of all his joys.

- **Be infinitely good, ...**

(Daughter: Dad! The man whom you want me to marry must be infinitely good.

Dad! Don't worry, but life will be enjoyable only if and his mother are infinitely poles apart.

Daughter: !!!)

Who can be infinitely good? Can one be infinitely good when infinitely hurt and humiliated, insulted and infuriated? Can one be infinitely good when left with devils infinitely bad?

Many good human beings live with absolutely no recognition just because they are infinitely good.

The research scholar wishes to carry out his research work under the guidance of a professor who must be infinitely good.

God is infinitely good and Man is infinitely ungrateful.

- **........raised us from the dust, and placed us here**

In all this happiness, who at his hand

Have nothing merited, nor can perform
Aught whereof he hath need: he who requires
From us no other services than to keep
This one.................................of all the trees
In Paradise that bear delicious fruit
So various, not to taste that only Tree
Of Knowledge, planted by the Tree of Life;
So near grows death to Life, ...

(God created us from the dust and placed us here amidst this happiness, though we have done nothing to deserve all this, nor indeed can we ever do anything He needs. God, in return of all this, requires nothing of us except to observe one command of His..... that of all trees that bear delicious fruits we should forbear to taste the fruit of only one tree, the Tree of Knowledge growing close to the Tree of Life.)

He raised us from the dust, but did not leave us in the dust, and did not remove from us happiness. It is Man who lives in the dust, polluting his heart, soul and mind and destroying his happiness by constantly using technology without caring a fig for the fellow human beings.

From who did Satan learn disobedience? He was obedient till Adam was created. Is it the power of Man, who could change even Satan's mind? Did Man think of teaching God knowledge by tasting the fruits from the Tree of Knowledge? Even today man is fond of doing something which he is instructed or advised not to do.

God placed Man in all happiness, but seeking more happiness, Man lost his happiness by disobeying the command of God. Even after paying a heavy price, man continues to be avaricious. Man is not happy even if both his hands overflow with currency notes, gold and diamond coins. He expects his hands to be made of gold and diamond or to be the currency, gold and diamond-making machines. God gave Man life, but Man gives life Death.

God requires from man no services. But man must realise that 'Service to humanity is service to God." In this fast moving world of technology, man keeps on running. He has no time to serve the fellow human beings.

- ....let us ever praise him, and extol

  His bounty, following our delightful task,
  To prune these growing plants, and tend these flowers;
  Which, were it toilsome, yet with thee were sweet."

(Let us praise him and admire his generosity that we enjoy after our day's delightful labour of pruning and tending these lovely flowers, a task, even if it were laborious, I should have enjoyed it in your company.)

We can ever praise one, but the person praised must be praiseworthy, we can extol one's bounty, but the person whose bounty is extolled must have self-contentment, but there can be none on earth, except God. So let us ever praise Him, and extol His bounty.

Task may be laborious, but must be delightful.

The poor gardener, after years of laborious tasks of pruning growing plants and tending flowers, died due to pains in his personal life.

Growing plants look more beautiful, but growing man?

Growing plants and blossoming flowers are testimonial to the taste of God, who deserves to be ever praised.

- To whom thus Eve replied: "O thou for whom

  And from whom I was formed, flesh of thy flesh,
  And without whom am to no end, my guide
  And head! What thou hast said is just and right.
  For we to him indeed all praise owe,
  And daily thanks; ....

(Did romantic dialogues start from Adam and Eve?

(Eve replied: "O Adam! For whom and from whose rib I was made, flesh of your flesh, and without whom I have no existence and who are my guide and mind. What you say is just right. We owe to God.)

The boy says to the girl, "You are the flesh of my flesh and bone of my bone."

Your happy breath makes my existence in this world meaningful.

Tom with his daily thanks finally betrayed all whom he thanked.

What you say may be just but not right, may be moral but not logical.

- **Mother of human race.**

(Eve is the mother of human race. If we knew the exact date of birth of Eve, Mother of human race, we could universally celebrate it as Mother's Day. The fell a prey to Satan's polished words and tasted the fruit from the Tree of Knowledge, forgetting or ignoring or not being conscious of the command of God, but the people of the world never thought of putting the blame on her for losing Paradise, perhaps because she is the Mother of human race. Prophet Muhammad says, "Paradise lies at the feet of one's mother." So the Paradise of the people of the world lies at the feet of Eve, for she is the Mother of human race.)

Just because Eve tasted the fruit of the Tree of Knowledge, we cannot leave the human race uncared.

Can Adam be called Father of human race?

Had Satan belonged to human race or been in possession of human virtues, he might not have spoiled the mind of the Mother of human race.

Will not God forgive the sins of the Mother of human race, and so the sins of all those who belong to human race?

Did the world come to know the value of 'Motherhood' from Eve, Mother of human race?

- …………………………to have thee by my side

Henchforth an individual solace dear:
Part of my soul, ……………………………

(Wife: You are part of my soul.

Husband: That's why I got paralytic attack.

Wife: !!!)

(A verbal fight between husband and wife (Both are M.A in English literature). Instead of shouting, abusing or physical force....they exchanged poems to each other as follows

Wife

I wrote your name on sand,

it got washed...

I wrote your name in air,

it was blown away.

Then, I wrote your name in my heart and got a heart attack.

Husband

God saw me hungry

He created Pizza.

He saw me thirsty

He created Pepsi.

He saw me in the dark.

He created light.

He saw me without problems

He created YOU.

Wife

Twinkle twinkle little star

You should know what you are.

And once you know what you are,

Mental hospital is not so far!.

Husband

The rain makes all things beautiful.

The grass and flowers too.

If rain makes things beautiful

Why doesn't rain on you?

Wife

Roses are red; Violets are blue;

Monkeys like you should be kept in zoo.

Husband

Don't feel so angry

You will find me there too

Not in a cage but laughing at too.

By having Sevathy by her side, Rni has earned enmity and hatred.

By having poets by his side, Tom became a great poet.

By having devils by the side, one cannot become an angel.

I told you that you were part of my soul and so my life has become partly lifeless.

Are your parents the main part of your life? Then you give your life Life.

- **How beauty is excelled by manly grace**

And wisdom, which alone is truly fair."

(Feminine beauty is excelled by manly grace and wisdom, the essence of true beauty.)

(Grace in heart means more than beauty on face. Who is the choice of a young boy for his marriage- a gracious girl? Or a beautiful girl? Does the boy look at her heart or face? The boy who marries a girl, the combination of Beauty, Grace and Wisdom is lucky. Is the beauty of a girl excelled by manly grace and wisdom? George Bernard Shaw was not good looking. Hearing of his knowledge and wisdom, a young and beautiful girl in full-make up, that to in the early morning of the day, went to Shaw's house and knocked at the door. When Bernard Shaw opened the door, the girl told him that her plan was to meet a fool at first in the morning. Shaw, on seeing her in full-make up, reminded of her seeing in the mirror her own face in the morning. Losing her face by the reply, the girl said to Shaw, "I am beautiful and you are intelligent. If we get married, our child will be as beautiful as I and as intelligent as you." Shaw asked her what would happen if the opposite were the result.)

The girl says that her beauty is excelled by manly grace.

She says, "How can I expect my beauty to excel when I live with a man who is not at all manly?."

In her quest and thirst for beauty, she lost her wisdom and Paradise as well.

He is wise but he is not too wise to know the value of wisdom.

By losing Paradise, did Man prove himself to be unwise?

• ....He, in delight

Both in her beauty and submissive charms,
Smiled with superior love, as Jupiter
On Juno smiles when he impregns the clouds
That shed May flowers, and pressed her matron lip
With kisses pure.

(Delighted with Eve's beauty and innocent charms, Adam smiled with the love of a superior person as Jupiter smiles on Juno when he impregnates the earth (representing Juno) with fertilizing showers of rain that produce May flowers, and imprinted pure kisses upon Eve's maiden lips.)

He smiles with superior love as Jupiter smiles on Juno.

When he pressed her matron lip with kisses, she might have the felt the pressure of pleasure.

Do not make kisses impure by pressing her matron lip before marriage.

Though superior love smiles at him, he considers himself inferior to the family that the girl he is in love with belongs to.

He says, "She is beautiful but she is never in her beauty."

The clouds shed May flowers on Adam and Eve but many couples have dark clouds surrounded and they find all flowers falling and withering.

• **Imparadised in one another's arms,**

The happier Eden, shall enjoy their fill
Of bliss on bliss; while I to Hell am thrust,

Where neither joy nor love, but fierce desire,
Among our other torments not the least,
Still unfulfilled, with pain of longing pines.

(These two are perfectly happy in each other's arms, which they find more blessed than Eden itself, and have in their life one joy continually succeeding another. On the contrary, I have been confined into Hell where there is neither joy nor love, but fierce, unfulfilled desires and painful longings which are not the least of my torments in Hell.)

The new couple is imprisoned in one another's hearts.

Every Romeo consider the heart of his Juliet his Eden.

The poor farmers are leading their lives with neither joy nor love.

All his long desires still remain unfulfilled.

Though his life is filled with bliss, he is yearning for hell-like life by marrying that worthless ghost.

- ....knowledge forbidden?

Only fruit was forbidden in Paradise, not knowledge.

If knowledge had been forbidden, Man might not have tasted the fruit of the forbidden Tree.

The poor farmer asks the Correspondent of the leading private school whether knowledge had been forbidden for his poor son in his school.

Neither knowledge nor any fruit is forbidden in Devil's paradise.

Despite forbidden knowledge, Man thinks of excelling God in knowledge.

- **The proof of their obedience and their faith?**

(Obedience can be proved and faith can be shown in innumerable ways, but how to trust one's obedience and faith? God looks at one's heart and He has the power to find out whether one is obedient and faithful. We all say that we obey the Lord and that we have faith in Him, but God knows everything. Before the creation of the first man, Adam, Satan was obedient and faithful, but his obedience and faith did not prolong when the Creator commanded him to bow before Adam. He disobeyed the command of God, saying the the creation of superior element could not bow before some inferior stuff. When a sick person refuses to consult a doctor due to his extreme faith in God, how could it be taken? When a scientist refuses to launch his rocket on a Tuesday on his firm belief that Tuesday is not a good day, how could it be taken? Can someone bow before his/her boss, can it be taken as a mark of obedience? When someone finds shelter in a place of worship during heavy rain or at the time of war, can his/her stay in the place of worship be considered 'Faith in the Lord'? Is it the proof of one's obedience and faith reliable? How long will one be obedient and faithful?)

The boss says to the employee that his bowing down cannot be considered a mark of humility.

The saint says, "Going to Masjids and Temples on Fridays and to Churches on Sundays is not the proof of Man's obedience to God or faith in Him."

Sevathan says, "I wash my wife's clothes every day and cook food, but she says that this is not the proof of my obedience."

The company needs not the proof of my ability, but the proof of my obedience and humility.

Pure heart is the proof of one's faith in God.

- ....I will excite their minds

With more desire to know, and to reject
Envious commands, invented with design
To keep them low, whom knowledge might exalt
Equal with gods.
(Knowledge might raise equal with gods.)
(This world filled with the so-called attractions excite the young minds with more desires to know and experience. Some just stop with 'knowing' and some risk with 'experiencing'. Is it Satan who

excite the young minds against God? Is it God's will that Man out of excessive desire must fall into the evil trap of Satan?)

Dr Shashi Tharoor excites innumerable minds across the world with his magnetic speech in British accent.

We desire to know more from his speech than from his deeds.

By rejecting envious commands, you have become closer to evil forces.

All his evil plans have been invented with designs.

You cannot keep yourself high by keeping others low.

You speak and act as though you were equal to gods in knowledge and power.

- **Short pleasures; for long woes are to succeed."**

Your short pleasures at the pain of others might give you long woes.

It is most unfortunate that Napoleon could not have even short pleasures at the end of his life.

Long woes disappeared by his short pleasures.

"Pleasure or pain, if life is short, what 's the use of talking about it?", says the Saint.

Life in this world will give you long woes, miseries without even some short pleasure, but not the life in the Next World.

Seeking some pleasures out of flirt, the teen-ager has lost his entire life.

- ....It was a rock

Of alabaster, piled up to the clouds,
(It was a high rock of alabaster that seemed to touch the sky.)

The prince's new bungalow has been built up with rocks of alabaster, piled to the clouds, but he is sleeping in a single and small room of his.

This eagle will carry you up even if you hide yourself somewhere inside some rock of alabaster, piled up to the clouds.

The mad man is so crazy and greedy that he wishes to commit suicide by jumping from the rock of alabaster, piled to the clouds.

His avariciousness made him climb up the rock of alabaster, piled up to the clouds, but he disappeared. He is found missing now.

- ....Gabriel sat

Chief of the angelic guards, awaiting night;

The rich politician is so arrogant that he might even expect Gabriel, Chief of the angelic guards, to be appointed as his personal guard.

The security awaiting night sleeps well during the day-time so as to discharge his duties at night.

The security sitting outside the large iron-gate of our bungalow with two umbrellas furled with one on the left and the other on the right reminds me of Gabriel, Chief of the angelic guards sitting.

The intention of Gabriel sitting, awaiting night is different from that of a young couple awaiting night.

The minister says that his guard guards him more perfectly than Gabriel, Chief of the angelic guards.

- ....one of the banished crew,

I fear, hath ventured from the Deep, to raise
New troubles: ....

(One of the fallen spirits that have ventured out of Hell to create some new mischief.)

(There is no need either for an angel or for any evil spirit to create in man's life new troubles. Mostly, we invite our own troubles. In the life parents, the troubles are the outcome of their own great expectations. Is there life without troubles?. The answer may be positive or negative, but man must know how to iron out the wrinkles in life. Man trusts someone and gets into new troubles. Man trusts even the corrupt and selfish politicians and invites troubles for the following five years. Man misuses technology and gets into trouble. Above all, the greedy nature of man lands him in many a trouble. Troubles are generally renewed or new troubles are generally raised in meetings conducted in many work places to maintain quality or to take some policy decisions. Just to make their presence well-felt, there are many who raise new troubles in meetings.)

Many new persons have been recruited in the company to raise new troubles.

When Man is an expert at raising new troubles, does Satan have any role?

The new manager is fond of new troubles.

Old troubles unsolved or unattended pave way for new troubles.

By raising new troubles, Satan makes man lose faith in the Lord.

• ....thy perfect sight

....

See far and wide.

(All are not saints that go to church, and all are not observers that see. What does 'perfect sight'? Teenagers have their answers direct or prevaricate. Saints have their own answers. They say that they see God and that their sight is perfect. But none has seen God. Once a believer asked his friend, a non-believer what he would do if he saw God. The non-believer replied that he would become a believer.

A boy fell in love with a girl, and he proposed his love to him many times. But all his proposals were rejected by the girl, for the girl had been told by one of her friends that the boy who was in love with him had a poor sight. Believing her words, the girl rejected him. But the boy did not give up his hope. His constant efforts yielded results. The girl, not out of love, but out of mercy told him that she would accept his love proposal, but on the condition that he must prove his 'perfect eye-sight' within a week. He made his own plan to prove his eye-sight. One day he went to a tree under the hot sun, hit a small nail on the tree and came back. The next day, in the evening, when it was getting dark, he asked the girl what she was able to see on the tree. The girl replied that she was able to see only the tree. The boy told her that he was able to see a small nail. Amazed at this, the girl told him that they could go near the tree and see the nail. Nodding his head, the boy went with her, but when he was moving towards the tree with the girl, he had a slip and fell down, for he could not see a buffalo lying on the way. Whether love is blind or not, the lover was blind.)

You have totally lost your sight, but you are talking about perfect sight.

His sight is perfect whenever he sees butterflies on roads.

The saint has lost his eye sight, but he with his mind perfectly sees far and wide.

Though young Tom's eye sight is perfect, what he sees will land him in troubles.

The Romeo of our street is ogling at young girls with his perfect eye sight but with imperfect mind.

- **Silence was pleased. Now glowed the firmament**

With living sapphires; ....
(In many houses, wives punish their husbands either by maintaining silence or by never maintaining silence. On many occasions, it is silence that pleases the life partners.)

(Silence was pleased with her song and now the sky glowed with living golden light.)

The greedy fellow says that he can live only with sapphires.

The husband says, "Oh, Silence! When will you come and dwell on my wife's tongue?."

Smiles will not make our MLA happy, but living sapphires.

The smile of the girl that I am in love with is costlier than sapphires.

Romeo says to Juliet, "I am reminded of ever living sapphires when I see your smiles."

- ....God hath set

Labour and rest as day and night, ...

(God hath set labour and rest as day and night; labour for the day and rest for the night. There are many who labour day and night and there are many who labour all days and rest all nights. But there are so many resting all days and nights. The importance of rest is felt only when one labours hard, but the delights of rest are experienced by those who never labour. In many houses, parents even at old age labour days and nights, converting their nights into days to give their children rest all days and nights. In work places, dedicated workers work beyond hours; those who work for salary work within hours and those who never consult their conscience act if they work. It is most unfortunate that luck on many occasions favours those who act as though they work. Believers do believe that they are being watched by the Lord all days and all nights. Fearing God, they labour hard, and to labour harder and harder, they rest at nights.)

God has set labour and rest as day and night; innocent man labours day and night and intelligent man rests day and night.

"In those days, there were plenty of dedicated teachers who laboured day and night till they lived, and they rested only in their graves", says the retired Headmaster.

The saint says, "Has God set labour for the poor and rest for the rich?."

The poor farmers say, "God has set upon us labour without rest and day without night."

"Daily wages for labour and high salary for rest" is the unwritten rule in many work places.

- ....other creatures all day long

Rove idle, unemployed, and less need rest;
Man hath his daily work of body or mind
Appointed, which declares his dignity,

And the regard of Heaven on all his ways;
While other animals unactive range,
And of their doings God takes no account.

(Other creatures, unlike man, roam idly all day alongwithout any work, and therefore need less rest. Man has his work to do daily, either physical or mental, and therein lies his dignity and Heaven's due recognition of all his activities. On the other hand, other animals roam about and God takes no cognizance of their actions.)

(Man has responsibilities. He, like other creatures, must avoid roaming about idly. Work, whether of body or mind, must be carried out with the sense of duty and dedication. Man thinks that woman has no work, but he does not know that kitchen is a battlefield wherein every woman struggles every day many times for the members of their families. To serve as a house wife is not easy. It is a woman who converts a house into home with her care, concern, love, affection, and above all, with her labour. There are some men who roam about like animals, and there are men who become animals. It is mainly by Labour Man declares his self-respect and dignity.)

Like other creatures, many of us rove idle, unemployed but need complete rest.

I have been doing a lot of work of body and mind and so I need some rest.

Man's dignity is in the work he executes with a sense of commitment.

The new GM works like a Trojan, but he expects all his doings to be taken account by God.

Man must declare his dignity by doing his daily work of body or mind.

The husband says, "My wife has no work either of body or of mind, but of her tongue that gets sharpened with harsh words, weakening my spirit and worsening my mind.

- **Unargued I obey;.......................................**

(An obedient servant can be an obedient master. Obedience is not slavery. By obeying others, one does not lose one's dignity or self-respect. Children are advised to obey their parents, teachers and the elders. All human beings are expected to obey the Creator. Man must never be ungrateful to the Creator. A good husband can expect his wife to love him, not to obey him. A wife can expect her husband to love her, not to obey her. Labourers can obey their bosses, but need not be their slaves. Slavery must be abolished. There are many labourers tolerating slavery for some pieces of bread. Humility should not turn out to be stupidity. Nowadays, the young students learn all lessons, except ethical values including obedience. Those were the days when children were afraid of their parents and teachers, and these are the days that parents and teachers are afraid of children.)

Do not use the word 'obey' when you do something after making arguments, making all feel exhausted with your arguments.

Unargued, the husband obeys the orders of his wife who is doing her PhD on male-chauvinism.

"Unargued, my son has never done anything", says Mohan to his friend.

Unargued, the lawyer won the case.

Unargued, I can obey your orders, but I am afraid of becoming dumb.

- **But neither breath of Morn, when she ascends**

  With charm of earliest birds; nor rising Sun
  On this delightful land; nor herb, fruit, flower
  Glistering with dew: nor fragrance after showers;
  Nor grateful Evening mild; nor silent Night,
  With this her solemn bird; nor walk by moon,
  Or glittering star-light, without thee is sweet.
  ..for whom
  This glorious sight, when sleep hath shut all eyes?"

(But neither the sift morning breeze, nor the chorus of birds in the morning, nor the rising sun lighting up the world, nor trees plants, fruits or flowers glittering with few drops, nor the fragrance of the earth after the showers of rain, nor easeful evening or silent night, nor the song of the nightingale, nor pleasant under moon-light or glittering stars have any pleasure for me without you. But what for the moon and the stars shine all through the night? What for is this beautiful setting when sleep has closed all eyes?")

Joe sleeps so soundly that his morning will not have its breath.

The poor farmers are leading breathless life in many places.

The Swamiji desires to live on the delightful land, enjoying all delights of life.

Mornings may lose their breath, summers their heat, spring their pleasantness, flowers their fragrance, soldiers their strength, rulers their concern, mothers their love, fathers their care, but can God lose His Grace and Mercy?

I need not look at the sky in search of glittering stars, but her eyes, I need not go near the flowers to smell its fragrance, but her nearness, I need not taste honey for taste but her words.

The devotees wish to have the glorious sight of the Creator but sleep caused due to the heavy mutton biryani shuts their eyes.

- **Shine not in vain, ………………………………**

The newly recruited candidate shines but in vain.

You can shine in any field but not in vain.

If a young employee shines, it pains the some of the seniors.

Samuel has been shining since he joined this institute but in vain.

By shining in vain, some of us are enjoying all privileges.

- **………………………………happy in our mutual help**

**And mutual love, the crown of all our bliss
Ordained by thee; and this delicious place,**

For us too large, where thy abundance wants
Partakers, and the uncropt falls to the ground
But thou hast promised from us two a race
To fill the Earth, who shall with extol
Thy goodness infinite, both when we wake,
When we seek, as now, thy gift of sleep. "

(The task assigned to us is the happiest bliss. We are thankful to you for assigning this beautiful place to us, which is too large for us, where there is such an abundant growth of fruits and flowers that they lie on the ground ungathered for want of more partakers. But we are happy to remember that you have promised from us two a whole human race to fill the earth. We and our progeny will ever praise you for your infinite goodness, both even when we wake and when we seek, as now, your blessed gift of sleep.)

There is no happiness in their mutual help.

There is mutual help but there is no mutual love between the husband and the wife.

The poor farmers tell the politician that his crown is full of their curses.

The poor girl tells her richest husband that his heart is a delicious and warm place for her to stay for ever.

The politician has decided to fill the earth with his own race in order to win the election.

The scholar says to his guide, "If Adam and Even had not filled the earth with his race, I would not have been suffering now, uploading assignments, publishing papers, taking the examinations, evaluating the scrips and buying your wife vegetables and teaching your children driving."

- **Ithuriel and Zephon, with wanged speed**

Search through this garden: leave unsearched no nook:
(Ithuriel and Zephon search through the whole garden swiftly and carefully without leaving any cook and corner.)

The police unstarched no nook but failed to catch the accused in the case.

Even if the police ,with wanged speed, searched through all the parks and the gardens of the city, they cannot identify the lovers.

The officers searched through the whole bungalow swiftly and arrested the corrupt minister, but he was released swiftly.

Only if you leave no nook and corner unsearched, you can arrest all the corrupt officers.

Even though the forest is thick with innumerable insects and serpents, the forest officers left unsearched any nook, but all their efforts ended up in smoke.

- **Like gentle breaths from rivers pure, thence raise**

  At least distempered discontented thoughts,
  Vain hopes, vain aims, inordinate desires,
  Blown up with high conceits engendering pride.

(Satan sought to infuse poison in her mind and to excite the animal spirit in her, that from the pure celestial spirit arises like soft breeze blowing from placid rivers. The fiend sought to taint her spirit by displeasure,discontentment, vain hopes and vain ambitions and inordinate desires, exciting high vanity and pride.)

Blown up with high conceits engendering pride, the new MD is changing the rules at the drop of a hat.

The child says, "My parents and teachers expect me to work like a Trojan, when I have vain hopes, vain aims and inordinate desires."

The priest is preaching of Contentment when he himself is in possession of discontented thoughts and earthly pleasure.

The speaker in his motivational speech just raises distempered discontented thoughts, vain hopes, vain aims.

Blown up with high conceits engendering pride, Arun is raising discontented thoughts and vain among his followers.

- ....the Prince of Hell;

(A pauper is far far better than the Prince of Hell. What pride is there in being the Prince of Hell? It is not the position that one holds matters, but the good service rendered to others. An honest pauper may not be prosperous but will lead a peaceful life, but a cruel, dishonest Prince of Hell may wallow in wealth but will be kept away from blessings. In Heaven, there is no place for the Prince of Hell. The poor may enter the Heaven easily but the rich cannot so easily enter the Heaven if God does not approve of the ways in which they earned money and bought properties. One should not become rich by making others poor. One should not become rich by cheating and exploiting others. The corrupt officers may live like a prince but would they be treated by God like a Prince on the Day of Judgment? It is a million dollar question. In a Tamil movie, the villain's popular dialogue is "I will be the bridegroom in a marriage, and I will be the dead body in a mourning house." Greedy people wish to be princes even in Hell. Hell or Heaven, they want power. Holding power is Responsibility, but being mad after power is Immaturity and Greediness.)

The saint says that a pauper of Heaven is better than a Prince of Hell.

One cannot expect the Prince of Hell to have his heart in the right place.

It is the extreme arrogance that has made him the Prince of Hell.

How can they work peacefully under the Prince of Hell?

All evil forces have joined together to torture all happily under the Prince of Hell.

• …………………………….Satan with contemptuous brow:

(with contempt in eyes)

(If Man goes closer to the Creator, Satan looks at him with contemptuous brow. When Satan's mercy and grace fall on Man, the Creator does not look at him with contemptuous brow, but has His sympathy for him. In some houses, when fathers look at their sons even casually, sons come to the conclusion that the fathers like Satan are looking at them with contemptuous brows. When students do not know the answers and do not behave well in class, teachers look at them with contemptuous brow. When a wife does not cook well, husband looks at her with contemptuous brow. When a husband does not wash clothes well, wife looks at him with contemptuous brow. When Romeo talks high of somebody's Juliet, own Juliet looks at him with contemptuous brow. Is looking at one with contemptuous brow the characteristic of Satan? Is Satan haunting the mind of Man so much?)

In films, the villains have to face everyone with contemptuous brows to become more famous than heroes.

The affectionate father says, "I do not know why my own son always looks at me with contemptuous brow."

The mother-in-law and the daughter-in-law are always looking at each other with contemptuous brow, and the only son lost his eye brows.

The team members say that whenever they see old Sevathy, they are reminded of Satan with contemptuous brow.

If you face the interviewers with contemptuous brow, how would they select you?

- ....who loves his pain?

(Is there anyone who loves pain? Motherly love is most trustworthy, but a mother does not want her children to have any pain. A mother loves pain when it can be transferred from her children to her. At the time delivery, mother's pain is most unbearable, but she bears it and loves it for the sake of her baby. Many of Romeos have their delights when their Juliets have pain, for it is a wonderful opportunity for Romeos to act if they were born on earth to bear the pain of their Juliets. Romeos who do not care a fig for their own mothers' pain will like a worm fallen into a frying pan, when their Juliets get a light headache. Romeos are willing to love and bear the pain of their Juliets, if and as long as their Juliets are beautiful. However, beauty lies in the eyes of the beholder.)

Before you love a girl, learn to love pain.

The saint has no pain for he loves pain.

No pain can pain me as I love pain.

The boy says to his girl friend, "Better to love pain than to love you."

How long can we be the lovers of pain?

- **Insulting Angel!**.................................

(A glorifying devil is better than an insulting angel. A devil may go higher in one's estimation by respecting others and an angel may down in one's estimation by humiliating or insulting others. But humiliating or insulting is the characteristic of an angel. When a devil praises one to the skies, it may have adverse effects. Some teenagers like to marry angels, though they are insulting. Some teenagers fall into the traps of devils looking like angels.)

The girl that I am in love with is, no doubt, an angel, but an insulting angel.

Better to marry a loving devil than to marry an insulting angel.

If she is so fond of insulting others, why should she be considered or called an angel.

The young romantic boy says to his parents, "The girl that I wish to marry is an insulting angel, but an angel."

Insulting or being insulted, an angel is an angel and a devil is a devil.

- **To settle here on Earth or in mid air;............**

There are many among us who are neither fit to settle here on earth nor in mid air.

He is such a business minded man that he would like to have his business in every nook and corner of this earth and in mid air too.

When he is without bottles, he is on earth; but after taking bottles, he would speak as if he were in mid air.

People are on earth, but the price of essential commodities is in mid air or in the sky.

People on earth vote for politicians and make them live in mid air.

• ....fit body to fit head!

(To make body fit, many teenagers are ready to walk from Kashmir to Kanyakumari. They are ready to perform gymnastics such as somersaults, rolls, and handsprings. But do they have hygienic food? Do they keep themselves free of tension, stress and nervousness? They want 'fit head', but they have attached their heads with ears. Their ears are found filled with earphones. Is there discipline in their life? Are they able to predict their future? Are they able to distinguish between what is right and what is wrong? Besides fit body and fit head, discipline is more important in one's life.)

Kannan has a body but not to fit his own head.

Joe has a fit body to perfectly fit his head.

Her head weighs heavier than her body because of her 'head weight'.

Such a peculiar shape Samuel has that neither his body nor his head fits him.

Your body is fit to fit a brainless head.

• **Your military obedience,**

(Nowadays many female research scholars wish to research on feminism, male chauvinism and gender studies. There are two major reasons, besides their own perceptions and interest. When they read some novels that deal with characters ill-treating their female counterparts, it creates negative impact in their minds. They consider the humiliation and ill-treatment experienced by some women somewhere or in a novel their own. The second reason is that in some or many houses, when men expect military obedience from women at home, they wish to find out a solution to male chauvinism. Military obedience is a must in an army, in a battlefield, but not at home.)

These are the days when people are more taken away by the flattering words in English of the so-called officers in power rather than the military obedience of the workers always toiling.

His obedience is military, but not his loyalty.

He got himself into military service with his military obedience.

Military discipline is more important than military obedience.

You were selected in the interview not because of your intelligence but because of your military obedience.

• ....Satan, alarmed,

Collecting all his might, dilated stood,
Like Teneriff or Atlas, unremoved:

(Satan stood alarmed, and, collecting all his might, expanded his body so much that he appeared like the peaks of Teneriff or Atlas, standing unshaken amidst them. Satan collects all his might from Man's weaknesses. If Man gets closer and closer to God, Satan might become weaker and weaker.)

The old Sevathy, like Satan, collected all her might to dislodge her enemies, arrogantly thinking that she could stand dilated like Teneriff or Atlas, unremoved, but she was defenestrated over night.

You can collect all your might and stand like Teneriff or Atlas, unremoved, and win your enemies in the battlefield, but you should not make Satanic or evil attempts.

The great warrior in every battlefield stood like Teneriff or Atlas, but he fell down miserably and could not stand even for seconds after his most trustworthy friends turning against him and shouting at him publicly.

The innocent man, though alarmed and capable of standing dilated like Teneriff or Atlas, did nothing to get things done.

You can stand dilated like Teneriff or Atlas when you face struggles and challenges in life, but not when you are standing in a queue to get a ticket from a cinema theatre ticket counter.

* **"Satan, I know thy strength, and thou know'st mine:**

   Neither our own, but given;.......................................
(Adam and Eve were not aware of their own strengths and weaknesses, and Eve failed to estimate Satan. Had Adam and Eve had, perhaps, been aware of Stan's strengths, they might have been careful. One must know one's own strengths and weaknesses. One's strength may someone else's weakness. A great warrior knows his own strengths and the strengths and weaknesses of his opponents. In interviews, "What are your strengths and weaknesses?" Is one of the questions raised. Eve's weakness turned out to be Satan's weakness, and Adam's weakness turned out to be Eve's strength. Eve's love for Adam was her strength, and Adam's love for Eve made him share the sin committed by his beloved wife. His love for his wife turned out to be his weakness. Would men have remained in Paradise, if Adam had not shared the sin?)

The main strength of Satan is on his tongue.

The husband prays; "Oh God! Thou gave the strength and intelligence to know the strength of Satan, but not that of my wife!."

The strength of mine is not my own, but given, and so is my weakness too.

He is such a bold man that he speaks anything and everything at any time but under the strength of his wife.